WORLD OF INSECTS

GRASSHOPPERS

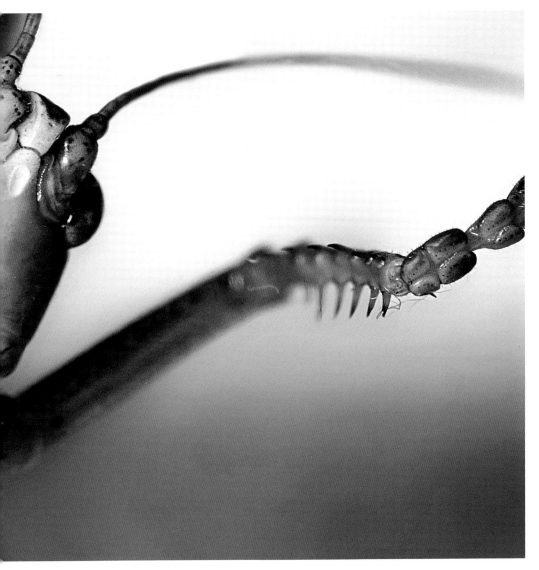

by Sophie Lockwood

Content Adviser: Michael Breed, Ph.D., Professor,
Ecology and Evolutionary Biology,
The University of Colorado, Boulder

THE CHILD'S WORLD®, MANKATO, MINNESOTA

Grasshoppers

Published in the United States of America by The Child's World®
1980 Lookout Drive • Mankato, MN 56003-1705
800-599-READ • www.childsworld.com

Acknowledgements!

The Child's World®: Mary Berendes, Publishing Director

The Creative Spark: Mary Francis, Project Director; Wendy Mead, Editor; Deborah Goodsite, Photo Researcher

The Design Lab: Kathleen Petelinsek, Designer, Production Artist, and Cartographer

Photos:

Cover: Reuters/Victor Ruiz/Landov; frontispiece and CIP: Comstock; title page: Anneke Schram/iStockphoto.com

Interior: Alamy: 14 (Gary Vogelmann), 24 (Reinhard Dirscherl); AP Photo: 33 (Schalk van Zuydam); Art Resource, NY: 28 (Victoria & Albert Museum, London); Corbis: 8 (Bettmann); Getty Images: 5, 10 (Abdelhak Senna/AFP), 34 (Chris Livingston); iStockphoto.com: 5, 23 (blindelinse), 36 (Ivan Chuyev); Landov: 31 (Reuters/Dwi Oblo); Lonely Planet Images: 30 (Juliet Coombe); Minden Pictures: 13 (Jef Meul/Foto Natura), 5, 18 (Frans Lanting); Oxford Scientific: 16 (Oxford Scientific), 21 (Larry F. Jernigan); Visuals Unlimited: 5, 27 (Gerold and Cynthia Merker).

Map: The Design Lab: 7.

Library of Congress Cataloging-in-Publication Data

Lockwood, Sophie.
  Grasshoppers / by Sophie Lockwood.
     p. cm.—(The world of insects)
  Includes index.
  ISBN-13: 978-1-59296-823-7 (library bound: alk. paper)
  ISBN-10: 1-59296-823-6 (library bound: alk. paper)
  1. Grasshoppers—Juvenile literature. I. Title. II. Series.
  QL508.A2L625 2007
  595.7'26—dc22   2007000173

TABLE OF CONTENTS

Chapter One

The Great Plains, 1874

Gray clouds gathered on the horizon. For farmers on the Great Plains, the approaching dark clouds might have carried much-needed rain. They did not. These clouds carried grasshoppers, millions upon millions of grasshoppers.

The grasshopper swarm blocked the sun. It swept across fields of corn, wheat, and millet, eating every plant down to the ground. Kitchen gardens, lush with tomatoes and beans and cabbages, became bare patches of earth in minutes. The locusts ate wool off live sheep and clothing off wash lines. Even the clothing on people was not safe from the ever-chewing insects. Paper, tree bark, leaves, wooden handles on hoes and shovels—nothing was safe from the greedy grasshoppers.

The grasshoppers invaded homes, crawled up pant legs, and flew down chimneys. Grasshoppers were several inches deep on the ground and, to warm themselves, they covered railroad tracks. When the trains tried to run, they could not because the tracks had

Did You Know?

According to *The Guinness Book of World Records*, the swarm of Rocky Mountain locusts, or grasshoppers, that attacked Nebraska from July 20 to July 30 in 1874 "covered an area estimated at 198,000 square miles (almost twice the size of Colorado). The swarm must have contained at least 12.5 trillion insects with a total weight of 27.5 million tons."[1]

1. Lisa Levitt Ryckman. "The Great Locust Mystery," http://www.denver-rmn.com/millennium/0622mile.shtml

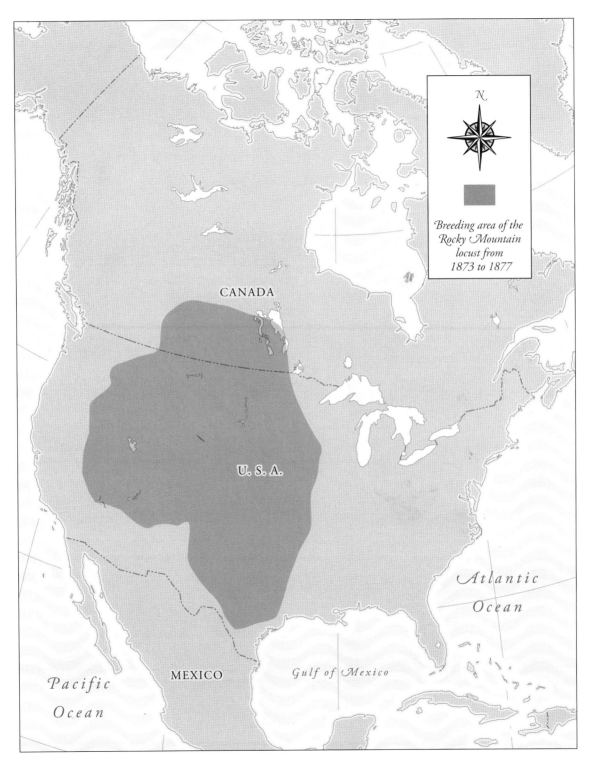

N

Breeding area of the
Rocky Mountain
locust from
1873 to 1877

CANADA

U.S.A.

Atlantic
Ocean

Pacific
Ocean

MEXICO

Gulf of Mexico

This map of the United States shows the breeding area of the Rocky Mountain locust from 1873 to 1877.

become slippery from the bodies of grasshoppers squashed on the tracks. For farmers and their families, people who depended on their crops to live, the grasshoppers became a cloud of doom. Many lost everything in a short time after the grasshoppers arrived on the wind.

The plague of grasshoppers was so terrible that the Kansas governor Thomas Osborn called a special session of the legislature. The government sold bonds and used the

There were so many grasshoppers all around that even the trains couldn't move.

money to help desperate farm families. Across the country, people sent money and supplies to help farmers in need.

Clever Kansans used their wits and developed inventions to deal with the grasshopper plague. One of the most significant was a grasshopper harvester— a large bulldozerlike blade—devised for scooping piles of grasshoppers off the ground.

The grasshopper plague of 1874 was followed by a worse plague two years later. Said one farmer from Saline County, Kansas, "Today, I lost sixty acres of wheat, eaten into the ground in less than an hour. I thought I had seen locusts two years ago, but I was mistaken. At about ten o'clock this morning, I noticed a heavy smoke rising in the West. . . . Soon the low hum, as of a distant threshing machine, filled the air. . . . Louder, louder, even louder the hum, till in a roar, the countless billions of devourers were on us, all around us. . . . Our garden is perfectly cleared; beans, cabbages, tomatoes, melons, everything utterly gone. The vines to the potatoes are gone, and I am expecting a boss [grass]hopper up here at any minute to request the loan of a spade to dig up my potatoes with."[2]

The grasshopper that plagued the Great Plains was the Rocky Mountain locust, a form of **migratory** grasshopper.

2. Lisa Levitt Ryckman. "Grasshopper Plagues and a Sense of Humor," http://ag.missouristate.edu/hoppstl.htm.

Grasshoppers still cause crop damage on North American farms, but nothing like the sky-blackening swarms of the 1870s. Today, the Rocky Mountain locust is extinct, and North America no longer has a grasshopper species that swarms in the numbers the Rocky Mountain locust did.

Although the Rocky Mountain locust is extinct, other kinds of grasshoppers, such as the pilgrim crickets shown here, can be just as destructive.

Chapter Two

The Grasshopper Cycle of Life

While their name implies that they inhabit grassy areas, grasshoppers can be found in many places. They eat plants for food. Grasshoppers are known as **herbivores**, or animals that eat plants. Most of them are not fussy about the types of plants they eat and will gladly devour cotton, corn, wheat, clover, low shrubs, and even tree bark.

Grasshoppers are found on every continent except Antarctica and in every climate zone except in polar regions. They live in fields, meadows, and anywhere with enough plant life to provide food. This includes rain forests, where grasshoppers, like tropical birds, may be brightly colored, in shades of blue, green, yellow, and red.

BODY PARTS

Grasshoppers, like other insects, have six legs and three body parts: head, **thorax**, and **abdomen**. Grasshopper legs are designed for jumping—one method of getting from one place to another. The hind legs are much longer than the two sets of front legs and come equipped with powerful muscles. One reason that grasshoppers can jump so far is that they have so little weight to carry, but strong legs certainly help.

Grasshoppers use all six legs when walking. The front legs also provide a means of holding onto food when eating. The hind legs are generally two to three times the length of the front legs and are thicker and more muscular.

A grasshopper's head contains eyes, mouthparts, and **antennae**. Grasshoppers have five eyes: two compound eyes called **ommatidia** and three small, simpler eyes known as **ocelli**. Compound eyes can see shape, color, and movement, and can determine distance. Simple eyes detect light and may help the grasshopper find the horizon, which helps when flying. Grasshopper mouthparts are simple in form and function. The **mandibles**, or jaws, are used to cut and grind. Palps are another part of the mouth and are used for touching, tasting, and determining temperature. Antennae are the grasshopper's main sense organs. With them, a grasshopper smells, touches, determines humidity, and senses wind speed and direction.

Wings and legs are attached to the thorax, the power plant of any insect. The strongest muscles lie in the thorax.

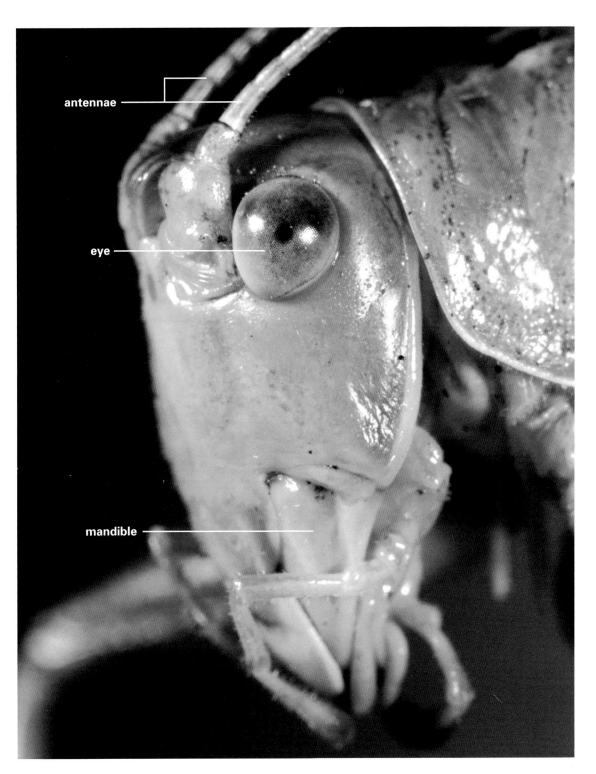

antennae

eye

mandible

The main parts of a grasshopper's head are its eyes, antennae, and mandibles.

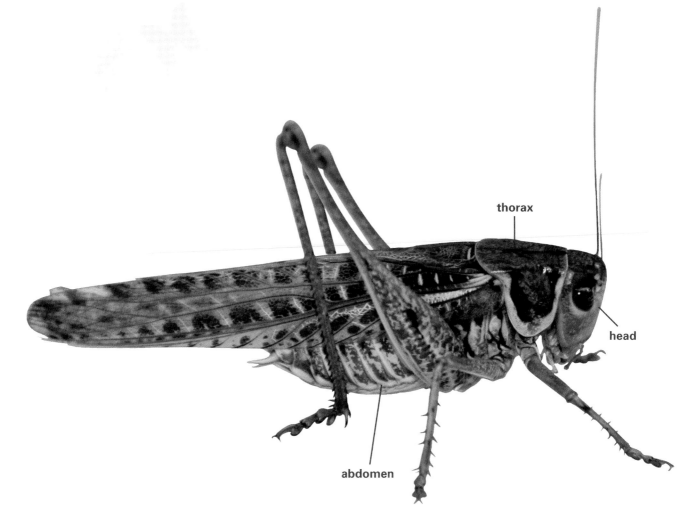

thorax

head

abdomen

Most grasshoppers have two pairs of wings that fold to cover the back, from the top of the thorax to the tip of the abdomen. Although many grasshoppers can fly, some have no wings and get around simply by hopping.

Grasshoppers breathe through tiny holes called **spiracles**, which are located along the thorax and abdomen. This is not at all like human breathing, since grasshoppers do not have lungs. Oxygen

A grasshopper has three main parts: the head, the thorax, and the abdomen

enters the grasshopper's body through the spiracles and is used up, and waste gases leave the body the same way.

A green fluid called **hemolymph** moves through the body along thin tubes. Hemolymph carries nutrients and body wastes, but it does not carry oxygen like human blood does. Hemolymph is pumped through the body by a very simple heart.

The abdomen holds a grasshopper's digestive and reproductive organs. Grasshoppers have a simple throat that sucks and swallows chewed plant matter. The nutrients from food are carried through the body in the hemolymph, and the waste is expelled through the anus.

THE LIFE CYCLE

Grasshoppers go through incomplete, or simple, **metamorphosis**. Unlike many other insects, they have only three stages of life: egg, nymph, and adult. Some grasshopper females deposit their eggs in the stems of plants, but most lay from 20 to 120 eggs beneath the soil in sacks shaped like pea pods. Once laid, the eggs are covered with a foam that hardens and protects the eggs. A female may lay three or four groups of eggs in different locations.

Did You Know?
Short-horned grasshoppers have their eardrums on their abdomens, just behind the hind legs. These eardrums sense sound vibrations.

In tropical regions, the eggs will hatch in three to four weeks. In colder climates, the eggs may wait over the winter before hatching. When they break through their eggs, the hatchlings are wormlike **nymphs**. As they grow, they will shed their skins several times. New skins are soft at first and harden when

Did You Know?
A grasshopper spends much more time as a nymph than it does as an adult.

Desert locust nymphs emerge from their eggs.

exposed to air. The process of shedding skins helps the nymphs' bodies grow. It takes 40 to 60 days for a nymph to become an adult. At that point, many species of grasshoppers have wings and can fly.

Adult grasshoppers usually live for two to five months. No rules fit every species of grasshopper. They vary in size, color, habitat, and even preferred foods. Many grasshoppers never eat a single blade of grass, and others eat nothing but grasses.

PREDATORS

Nature allows insects to produce young in huge numbers because the chance of an insect egg surviving to adulthood is slim. Many predators eat grasshoppers at any stage of development: egg, nymph, or adult.

Birds are major insect eaters, and storks love dining on grasshoppers. A single stork can eat up to 1.8 kilograms (4 pounds) of grasshoppers in a day. Grasshopper sparrows, small as they are, thrive on a diet of grasshoppers, snails, and other insects.

Reptiles, amphibians, and many mammals—including humans—eat grasshoppers because they are a nutritious,

healthy food. Grasshoppers are loaded with protein. Grasshopper mice, for example, practically live on these insects. Grasshoppers make up about 80 percent of the mice's diet.

Other insects also prey on grasshoppers. The long, green praying mantis will crunch its way through several grasshoppers a day. Other insects that feast on grasshoppers include jumping spiders, wolf spiders, robber flies, and tiger beetles. A company of South American army ants can dismantle a large katydid—a type of grasshopper—in seconds and haul the body parts back to the bivouac, or temporary shelter, to feed the other ants.

A chameleon snacks on a grasshopper.

Chapter Three

Grasshoppers, Grasshoppers, and More Grasshoppers

Three hundred million years ago, grasshoppers flew, leapt, and munched in the great forests that existed during a time known as the **Carboniferous** Period. Fossils of early grasshoppers have been found preserved in stone and amber. These ancient relatives of modern grasshoppers were not much different in size or shape from the modern versions.

Most grasshoppers are active by day, flying and feeding in the bright summer sun. There are only about 200 nocturnal species of grasshoppers, which are active at night and live in rotting wood or dead leaves. One such species is the Jerusalem cricket (actually a

Did You Know?
The world's largest grasshopper is the *Tropidacris latreillei* that lives in Venezuela and Colombia. This 13-centimeter (5-inch) grasshopper is toasted and eaten by the people of the Yukpa-Yuko tribe.

wingless grasshopper) that burrows into loose, sandy soil along the Pacific Ocean in North America.

Because so many species of grasshoppers are daytime feeders, they need a number of defenses against predators. **Camouflage** is one method of defense. Many grasshoppers are pure green and, placed against green leaves, disappear into the background. Desert-dwelling grasshoppers are generally speckled like the desert floor. Mimicking other objects, such as twigs, stones, and bird droppings, is another grasshopper defense.

Warning coloration and group living conditions help preserve grasshopper species. Many grasshoppers thrive on toxic leaves, making themselves foul-tasting or poisonous to predators. The coloring of a rain forest grasshopper, with its bright blue, red, yellow, and green, tells hungry creatures, "Don't eat me! I taste horrible!" Many of these grasshopper species live in clusters, which is a kind of protection of its own. When a bird samples one grasshopper in a group and it tastes bad, it leaves the others alone.

Some grasshoppers are equipped with more active defense systems. They have spines on their hind legs that deliver a painful jab. Others, like the Mexican *Taeniopoda auricornis,* startle

Did You Know?
The world's smallest grasshopper is the *Lithidium pusillium,* a tiny South African grasshopper that measures 1 to 2 millimeters (0.04 to 0.08 inches) long.

potential predators. They flash their wings and chase danger away.

TYPES OF GRASSHOPPERS

Grasshoppers come in one of three varieties: short-horned, long-horned, and pygmy. Most species belong to the family Acrididae (ah-KRIHD-ih-dee), the short-horned grasshoppers, which contains 10,000 to 11,000 species.

A short-horned grasshopper hides from its predators by blending in with its environment.

Desert Grasshoppers

In the Sonoran Desert, small, short-horned grasshoppers leap between scruffy bushes and spiny cacti. While it might seem that a desert would not have enough plant food for them, grasshoppers are common insects seen on a desert hike. One reason grasshoppers thrive in desert climates is that most are not picky eaters. They will eat a varied mixture of shrubs, wildflowers, and grasses.

Many desert grasshoppers are banded or speckled with brown, black, white, or reddish colors. Sitting on the ground, they become almost invisible. Others blend in with the shrubs they feed on. Gray bird grasshoppers and their close cousins, green bird grasshoppers, perch on one plant all day and blend in with the leaf coloring. Creosote bush grasshoppers, for example, are olive green with shiny, pearl white spots and look very much like creosote leaves.

Large horse lubber grasshoppers and harlequin grass-hoppers don't worry about blending in with the scenery. Both of these brightly colored species taste terrible. Their colors warn predators to stay away.

The antennae on these grasshoppers are usually equal to about half the length of the insect's body. Short-horned grasshoppers are the most recognized grasshoppers because they include swarming species called locusts.

Long-horned grasshoppers, Tettigoniidae (teh-tih-go-NY-id-dee), include 6,800 species of grasshoppers, katydids, and bush-crickets. These insects are more closely related to

A long-horned grasshopper rests on a flower.

crickets than to grasshoppers and can be identified because their antennae are roughly as long as their bodies. Most of these species eat leaves, flowers, bark, and seeds, but some will also eat other insects, snails, and even tiny snakes.

The smallest group of grasshoppers is Tetrigidae (teht-TRIH-jih-dee), or pygmy grasshoppers. This small family lives in tropical forests and includes about 1,400 species. Most of these grasshoppers measure less than 2 centimeters (0.75 inches) in length.

Phymateus leprosus *is a member of Tetrigidae family and is not usually more than 2 centimeters (0.75 inches) long.*

Chapter Four

In Appreciation of Grasshoppers

The Yaquis, a Native American group from Sonora, Mexico, tell a legend of a cricket and a grasshopper. This story has been passed down from generation to generation.

A cricket invited a grasshopper to join him for dinner. "Let's go to the feast together and have a wonderful time." The two arrived at the dinner and ate, drank, and had great fun.

When they left the banquet, they walked along the edge of the grasslands. They came upon a sleeping mountain lion and climbed up on the big cat and sang. It is the nature of both crickets and grasshoppers to sing the night away, particularly when it is warm, and this night was very warm. The very tired lion grew angry when the cricket and grasshopper woke him. He rose up and tried to walk away from the irritating noise.

Unfortunately, the lion could not escape the chirping insects. The insects kept up their endless singing all night long. They moved down the lion's back and onto its tail. Finally, the lion could take no more. It flicked its long tail and away flew the insects. The lion climbed up on a rocky ledge to finish its rest, while the cricket and grasshopper landed in the grass and stayed there.

Even today, the mountain lion knows not to sleep where crickets and grasshoppers chirp loudly all through the night.

Many cultures find lessons in nature, and grasshoppers seem to be a popular subject. Grasshoppers are matched up with toads, coyotes, and meadowlarks in folktales that teach life lessons. The most famous fable about grasshoppers deals with busy ants and a lazy grasshopper. In this fable by Aesop, the ants collect and store food for the winter, while the grasshopper does nothing but sing and relax all summer. Winter comes, and the grasshopper is left with

no food or shelter, while the industrious ants are cozy and well fed in their hill. Clearly, Aesop did not know that grasshoppers are short-lived, and only their eggs survive through the winter.

Grasshoppers, such as this painted grasshopper, have appeared in many fables and legends.

Grasshoppers and locusts appear frequently in the Bible. The Old Testament encourages people to eat grasshoppers, locusts, and katydids. It also tells the story of Moses asking the Egyptian pharaoh to free the Jewish slaves. When the pharaoh refuses, a plague of locusts descends on Egypt. In another story found in the Bible, John the Baptist survived living in the desert by eating locusts and honey.

Would You Believe?
When grasshoppers are picked up, they "spit" brown liquid that is known by most people as "tobacco juice." Scientists believe that this liquid may protect grasshoppers from attacks by ants and other insects.

An illustration shows Moses and the plague of locusts.

Proverbs and sayings apply grasshopper characteristics to bits of wisdom. Africans say, "Do not send an elephant to catch grasshoppers," which means that people should use the correct tool to do a job. A Chinese proverb warns that, "The mantis seizes the locust but does not see the yellow bird behind him."

FOOD FOR THE HUNGRY

In North America, people do not think of insects as suitable food. Many others would disagree with this opinion, however. For millions of hunter-gatherers today, grasshoppers make excellent meals and serve as a standard part of daily nutrition. Grasshoppers have only 6 percent fat, and that fat is unsaturated, so it is healthier than the fat found in beef, chicken, or pork.

Few North Americans would consider eating grasshoppers on a regular basis, but this has not always been true. Long before Europeans came to the Americas, native peoples collected and cooked grasshoppers as part of their diet.

The Paiute of Nevada hunted grasshoppers by digging trenches and covering them with straw. They herded grasshoppers into the trenches, lit the straw on fire, and ground

the charred grasshoppers into meal. The high-protein meal was used in the same way cornmeal or other flour might be used.

Many ethnic cuisines offer bugs on the menu, and dining on grasshoppers is a gourmet treat. In Japan, fried rice-field grasshoppers, called *inago,* are considered a delicacy. In South America, native peoples capture the slow-moving lubber grasshoppers and

Did You Know?
Grasshoppers symbolize nobility and prosperity in some Asian art. The Chinese consider the grasshopper to be the symbol of rebirth or everlasting life.

A Chinese market sells locusts along with other foods.

toast them over an open fire for a snack as tasty as popcorn—and far healthier. In Thailand, grasshoppers are served stir-fried, roasted, or heavily spiced. Sakon Nakhon, a research center in Thailand, packages and ships edible insects world-wide. Grasshoppers come already cooked and salted—just open the can and enjoy!

A boy sells grasshoppers as a snack in Indonesia.

Chapter Five

Man and Grasshoppers

The battle between humans and grasshoppers stretches back to biblical times, and the battle is not over. Humans have not won. Small populations of local grasshoppers damage crops on every continent except Antarctica. The worst damage comes when large numbers of grasshoppers gather in one place—a plague of locusts.

Each year for the past fifty or so years, African farmers, shepherds, and goatherds have looked to the sky with dismay as new swarms of desert locusts sweep across Morocco or Algeria, from Nigeria to the Sudan and onward to Ethiopia and Uganda.

According to the United Nations Food and Agriculture Organization, desert locusts are a massive, expensive problem. They eat millions of dollars worth of crops, fruit, wool, and even the tents nomadic people live in. A large swarm of locusts may contain 50 billion insects. That equals roughly

50 million per square kilometer (20 million per square mile)—a horde of insects that eats as much food in one day as do all the people in New York, Los Angeles, Dallas, Miami, Chicago, Boston, and some of those cities' suburbs.

Trying to control the insects costs billions of dollars for pesticides, spray planes, research, and manpower. In an effort to

Did You Know?
Swarming grasshoppers have been known to eat saddles, shoes, and other leather products.

A swarm of locusts fills the sky near Dakar, Senegal.

keep locusts from causing so much damage, scientists have investigated why swarms develop. Oddly enough, swarming is *not* normal for desert grasshoppers. Usually, they live individual lives, feeding on local plant life.

Breeding conditions need to be perfect to create a swarm. When the weather, ecology, and food supply are ideal, females mate and lay their eggs. With these ideal conditions, the eggs hatch and develop into nymphs. It may take months before the locusts are ready to swarm. They wait until their group is large enough, and then they move as one.

Lahbib Bouhabs, a Moroccan farmer and father of eight children, said, "Around two o'clock big, big swarms

A Florida scientist studies the giant grasshopper, which has attacked parts of his state.

came in and when they saw the vegetation they landed. If it had been a month earlier it would have been disastrous as I had five hectares of wheat in the field. As it was they destroyed 104 almond trees and 70 olive trees."[3]

DIFFICULT DECISIONS

Many international groups and government agencies spray pesticides to fight the swarms. The pesticides, however, do not always work, and they can cause other problems. For one thing, grasshoppers are a food source for thousands of people living in locust-damaged areas surrounding the Sahara and in the Middle East. Spraying pesticide kills the grasshoppers, but it also poisons the food supply.

All of nature is involved in a cycle. Other animals that feed on poisoned grasshoppers take in the pesticide. The pesticide may not kill those animals directly, but other problems might occur. Some birds that eat too much pesticide lay damaged eggs or stop laying eggs altogether. Lizards, toads, and other reptiles eat poisoned grasshoppers and, in turn, also become poisoned. The poison spreads up the food chain. In addition, pesticide seeps into the soil. When the chemicals are dissolved in water, local plants suck up those chemicals, and crops may become contaminated.

3. FAO Newsroom, "Counting the Human Cost," http://www.fao.org.

NEW WAYS TO CONTROL GRASSHOPPERS

One key element in controlling grasshopper populations in general, and local swarms in particular, is identifying where they lay their eggs. Scientists know what conditions are necessary for the large-scale production of young, so they watch potential breeding sites carefully. When grasshopper nymphs hatch, scientists monitor their progress. If a swarm develops, it can be tracked by a global-positioning satellite so pesticides can be sprayed over a smaller area.

Would You Believe?
In the heart of the Beartooth Mountain Range in Montana, a glacier has been slowly melting for years. Embedded in the ice are millions of grasshoppers, caught by the wind and blown into the mountains in about 1600. The grasshoppers have been identified as Rocky Mountain locusts, a species that is now extinct.

Scientists are studying ways to control the size of grasshopper populations.

New forms of pesticides and biological controls are being investigated regularly. Scientists are working on creating pesticides that do not pollute the soil but are effective in stopping swarms.

Scientists also experiment with biological controls, animals or plants that decrease grasshopper populations. Tiny animals (protozoa) make some grasshoppers sick and destroy the population. Fungus and a type of wasp are being used to try to control the number of grasshoppers in the western United States. When sprayed on the plants grasshoppers eat, specific types of fungi cause grasshoppers to die. Certain wasps also attack the grasshoppers by laying their eggs on them. The wasp larvae eat their grasshopper hosts alive, reducing the population. This may also increase the wasp population, however, possibly creating a different problem.

Attempts to defeat grasshoppers have had limited success. Perhaps the best solution is to harvest the grasshoppers or locusts and use them for food. Grasshoppers could feed many of the starving people in Africa and Asia. Any surplus in the harvest could be marketed to gourmet restaurants throughout the world, providing profit in place of the devastating loss that usually accompanies a swarm of locusts.

Glossary

abdomen (AB-doh-men) the elongated portion of the body of an arthropod, located behind the thorax

antennae (an-TEN-nee) thin, sensory organs found on the heads of many insects

camouflage (KAM-oh-flahj) protective coloring that allows an animal or plant to blend in with its surroundings

Carboniferous (kar-boh-NIFF-fuhr-us) a geologic period from 362.5 million to 290 million years ago

hemolymph (HEE-moh-lymf) a bloodlike fluid in the bodies of many invertebrates

herbivores (ER-bih-vohrz) animals that only eat plants

mandibles (MAN-dih-bulz) the jaw parts of an insect's mouth

metamorphosis (meht-uh-MOR-foh-sis) a complete change in body form as an animal becomes an adult

migratory (MY-greh-toh-ree) moving from one region to another

nymphs (NIMFS) insects in the stage of development between egg and adult

ocelli (oh-SELL-eye) simple eyes

ommatidia (ahm-uh-TIH-dee-uh) the visual facets, or lenses, of an insect eye

spiracles (SPEER-uh-kulz) small openings in the side of an insect, used for breathing

thorax (THOR-aks) the middle division of an insect, crustacean, or spider

For More Information

Watch It

Basic Facts about Insects, DVD and VHS. (Huntsville, TX: Educational Video Network, Inc., 2004.)

Life in the Undergrowth, DVD. (Burbank, CA, BBC Video, 2006.)

Natural History: Insects and Arachnids, DVD. (Orlando, FL: A2ZCDS.com, 2005.)

Read It

Blobaum, Cindy. *Insectigations: 40 Hands-on Activities to Explore the Insect World*. Chicago: Chicago Review Press, 2005.

Greenaway, Theresa. *Big Book of Bugs*. New York: DK Publishing, 2000.

McDonald, Mary Ann. *Grasshoppers*. Chanhassen, MN: The Child's World, 2006.

Miller, Sara Swan. *Grasshoppers and Crickets of North America*. Danbury, CT: Franklin Watts, 2003.

Squire, Ann O. *Crickets and Grasshoppers*. Danbury, CT: Children's Press, 2004.

Winner, Cherie. *Everything Bug: What Kids Really Want to Know About Insects and Spiders*. Minnetonka, MN: NorthWord Press, 2004.

Look It Up

Visit our Web site for lots of links about grasshoppers:
http://www.childsworld.com/links

Note to Parents, Teachers, and Librarians: We routinely verify our Web links to make sure they are safe, active sites—so encourage your readers to check them out!

The Animal Kingdom
Where Do Grasshoppers Fit In?

Kingdom: Animal

Phylum: Arthropoda

Class: Insecta

Order: Orthoptera

Major families: Acrididae, Tettigoniidae, Tetrigidae

Index

About the Author
Sophie Lockwood is a former teacher and a longtime writer. She writes textbooks, newspaper articles, and magazine articles. Sophie enjoys writing about animals and their habits. The most interesting part of her research, Sophie says, is learning how scientists apply their knowledge to save endangered species. She lives with her husband in the foothills of the Blue Ridge Mountains.